Creeping Caterpillars

by Robin Nelson

first step nonfiction

Lerner Publications ◆ Minneapolis

Copyright © 2017 by Lerner Publishing Group, Inc.

The images in this book are used with the permission of: © chinahbzyg/Shutterstock.com, p. 4; © Pabkov/Shutterstock.com, p. 5; © wonderisland/Shutterstock.com, p. 6; © Samet Guler/Shutterstock.com, p. 7; © BHJ/Shutterstock.com, p. 8; © iStockphoto.com/Shaun Wilkinson, p. 9; © David Wrobel/Visuals Unlimited/Getty Images, p. 10; © iStockphoto.com/Diana Meister, p. 11; © iStockphoto.com/lmjp, p. 12; © phichet chaiyabin/Shutterstock.com, p. 13; © Nopporn Chainate/Shutterstock.com, p. 14; © Survivalphotos/Alamy, p. 15; © Katarina Christenson/Shutterstock.com, p. 16; © ChameleonsEye/Shutterstock.com, pp. 17, 21; © Donald Specker/Animals Animals, p. 18; © hwongcc/Shutterstock.com, p. 19; © Steven Russell Smith Photos/Shutterstock.com, p. 20; © Bildagentur Zoonar GmbH/Shutterstock.com, p. 22.
Front cover: © TTstudio/Shutterstock.com.

Main body text set in ITC Avant Garde Gothic Std Medium 21/25.
Typeface provided by International Typeface Corp.

Lerner Publications Company
A division of Lerner Publishing Group, Inc.
241 First Avenue North
Minneapolis, MN 55401 USA

For reading levels and more information, look up this title at www.lernerbooks.com.

Library of Congress Cataloging-in-Publication Data

Names: Nelson, Robin, 1971– author.
Title: Creeping caterpillars / Robin Nelson.
Description: Minneapolis : Lerner Publications, [2016] | Series: First Step Nonfiction. Backyard critters | Audience: Ages 5–8. | Audience: K to grade 3. | Includes index.
Identifiers: LCCN 2015035211| ISBN 9781512408805 (lb : alk. paper) | ISBN 9781512412178 (pb : alk. paper) | ISBN 9781512409987 (eb pdf)
Subjects: LCSH: Caterpillars—Juvenile literature. | Butterflies—Development—Juvenile literature.
Classification: LCC QL544.2 .N435 2016 | DDC 595.7813/92—dc23

LC record available at http://lccn.loc.gov/2015035211

Manufactured in the United States of America
1 – CG – 7/15/16

Table of Contents

Caterpillar Bodies

Caterpillars have long, squishy bodies.

This caterpillar creeps across a branch.

They have many little legs to help them crawl.

Some caterpillars are hairy.

Some are not.

Stripes, dots, and bright colors scare other animals away.

Caterpillars can have stripes or dots.

A small caterpillar crawls on a leaf.

Caterpillars can be big or small.

Caterpillars have 12 eyes! Some are so small you may not see them.

Caterpillars have tiny, **beady** eyes.

They have strong mouths
for eating.

Where to Find Caterpillars

Caterpillars live wherever there are plants to eat.

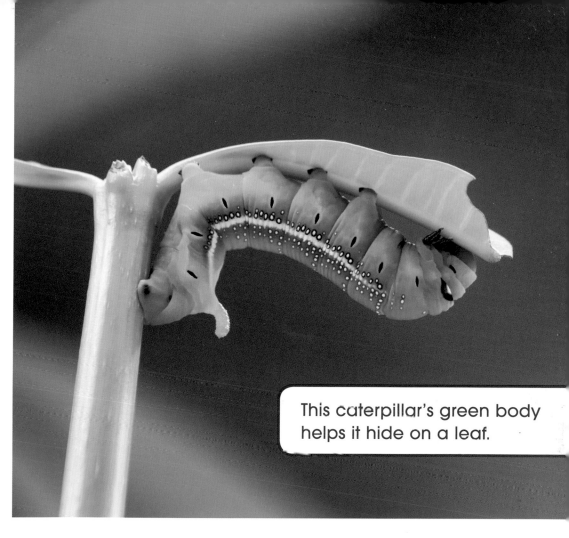

This caterpillar's green body helps it hide on a leaf.

They often hide under leaves.

13

Munch, munch, munch.
Caterpillars eat a lot!

Caterpillars hatch from eggs and eat them!

First, they eat their **eggshells**. Then they eat leaves.

They crawl from leaf to leaf
and keep on eating.

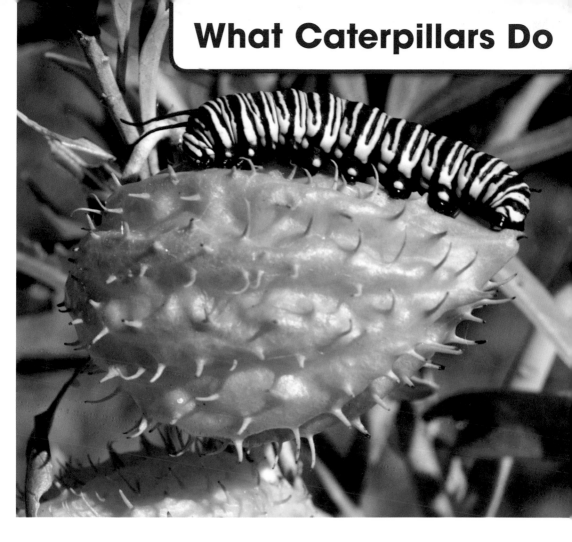

Eating so much helps caterpillars grow.

These caterpillars are wiggling out of their skin.

Their skin gets tight.
They wiggle out of it!

Caterpillars molt four or five times.

Wiggling out of their skin is called **molting**.

Caterpillars build **cocoons**.

Soon they turn into butterflies or **moths**!

Caterpillar Parts

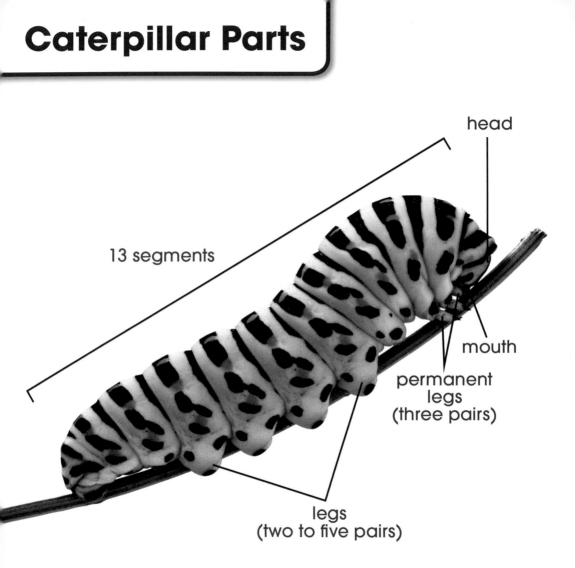

head

13 segments

mouth

permanent
legs
(three pairs)

legs
(two to five pairs)

Glossary

beady – small and round

cocoons – coverings that protect insects while they grow and change

eggshells – the outside of eggs

molting – losing old skin

moths – insects that are like butterflies but fly at night and are less colorful

Index